Luisa Rose
Blumenfeen
Ausmalbuch für Erwachsene

Bibliografische Information der Deutschen Nationalbibliothek:
Die Deutsche Nationalbibliothek verzeichnet diese Publikation in der Deutschen Nationalbibliografie; detaillierte bibliografische Daten sind im Internet über http://dnb.dnb.de abrufbar.

© 2016 Luisa Rose; 1. Auflage
Covergrafik, Texte & Illustrationen © 2016 Luisa Rose

Herstellung und Verlag: BoD – Books on Demand, Norderstedt

ISBN: 9783743137738

COMMON PLANTAIN
(Plantago Major)

Common Plantain thought he'd play
Around the house one summer day;
Gardener called him "Naughty Weed!"
Which made him very sad indeed!

DOWNY YELLOW VIOLET
[*Viola Pubescens*]

Downy Yellow Violet said,
"My woodland sister droops her head;
But I go romping on my way,
My face up turned to greet the day."

QUEEN ANNE'S LACE
[*Daucus Carota*]

The fairy babies simply race
Each night to Madame Queen Anne's Lace,
Cuddled so warmly to her breast
She gives each babe a good night's rest.

YELLOW ADDER'S TONGUE
[*Erythronium Americanum*]

By dainty Yellow Adder's Tongue
Such fairy elfin songs are sung
That fairy folk come trooping out
To hear what it is all about!

RHODODENDRON
[*Rhododendron Maximum*]

Rhododendron came to town
In her green and rose pink gown;
She's so pretty that we give
Her the nicest spots to live.

LAMB-KILL
[*Kalmia Augustifolia*]

Lamb-Kill's as pretty as can be;
He can't be trusted though, you see,
He's mischievous, and feeds the sheep
Some sort of stuff that makes them sleep.

CANADA LILY
[*Lilium Canadense*]

Canada Lily grows quite wild
But she's a gentle graceful child,
She loves the meadows where she plays
Happily through the summer days.

CREAM-CUP
[*Platystemon Californica*]

Cream-Cup comes, the pretty thing,
To gladden California's Spring,
You'll meet them everywhere in flocks
Clambering over hills and rocks.

BABY BLUE EYES
[*Nemophila Insignis*]

Baby Blue Eyes comes in Spring
Dainty dimpled smiling thing;
Calls to us from far away,
"Won't you please come out to play?"

CALIFORNIA LARKSPUR
[*Delphinium Americanum*]

California Larkspur plays
With Golden Poppies all his days,
Prettiest children ever seen
Dressed in gold and blue and green.

WILD MORNING GLORY
[*Convolvulus Sepium*]

Wild Morning Glory runs away
Along the woodland paths to play;
She climbs about with easy grace
And hangs her bright bells every place.

CARDINAL FLOWER
[*Lobelia Cardinalis*]

Stately Madame Cardinal Flower
Holds receptions by the hour;
Invites those whom she likes the best,
And Humming Bird's her favorite guest.

TURKS CAP LILY
[*Lilium Superbum*]

Said Turks Cap Lily, "As you see
I'm as industrious as can be;
That's why I'm rich, and can afford
To give such swarms of bees their board."

WILD COLUMBINE
[*Aquilegia Canadensis*]

"I keep my sweets," said Columbine,
"For Humming Bird, a friend of mine;
He comes at sun-down every night,
And is *so* grateful and polite."

WHITE CLOVER
[*Trifolium Repens*]

The Robin heard white Clover say,
"When I'm grown I'll be Sweet Hay,
To feed the cow so she can give
Nice milk to help wee children live."

EVENING PRIMROSE
[Onogra Biennis]

Said Evening Primrose, "I wake up,
When twilight comes, and fill my cup
With sweetest honey for my friends
The moths, who come when day-time ends.

WILD GERANIUM OR CRANESBILL
[*Geranium Maculatum*]

Along the wooded roads I grow
And children pluck me as they go,
And say my flowers are sweet and gay,
Which makes me happy all the day.

FIREWEED
[*Epilobium Augustifolium*]

When fire fiends through the woodland race
Leaving a blackened barren place,
Then Fire Weed knows that it's his duty
To make the burned land bloom with beauty.

LUPINE
[*Lupinus Perrenis*]

In sand dunes hot or meadows gay
The little Lupines love to play;
In dainty gowns of violet blue
They'll nod a glad "Good-day" to you.

DUTCHMAN'S BREECHES
[*Dicentra Cucullaria*]

The daintiest twins in all the land,
Dutchman's Breeches, hand in hand,
In Springtime tumble down the hill
Just like another Jack and Jill.

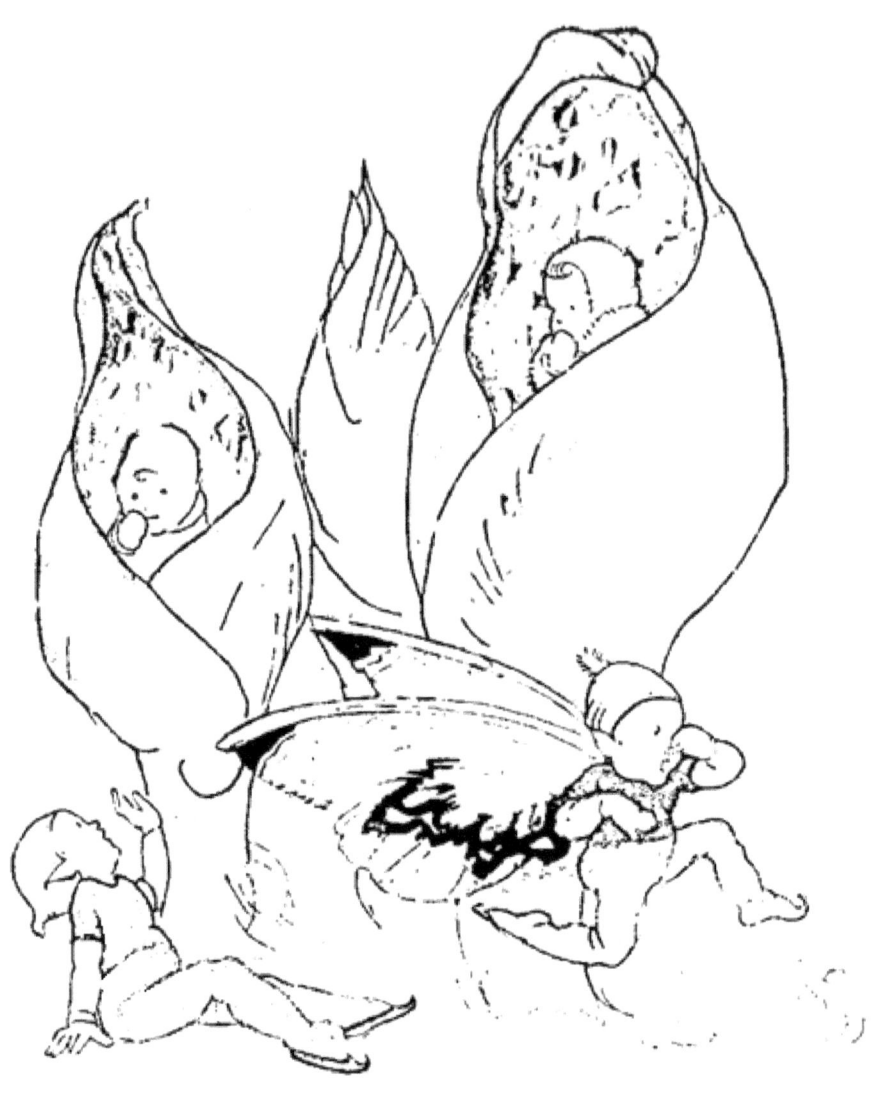

SKUNK CABBAGE
[*Symplocarpus Foetidus*]

Skunk Cabbage is a handsome thing
Comes while it is cold in Spring;
Protects his babes from wind and storm
In a big coat that keeps them warm.

JACK IN THE PULPIT
[*Arisaema Triphyllum*]

Each Sunday, on a mossy mound,
The Flower Children gather round
Jack-In-The-Pulpit, while he teaches
Each one, to practice what *he* preaches.

BLUE FLAG
[Iris Versicolor]

Blue Flag's as pretty as can be;
Cousin to Mam'selle Fleur De Lis;
Loves cool damp places, and is fond
Of living near a stream or pond.

PEARLY EVERLASTING
[*Anaphalis Margaritacea*]

Around the hillsides in the sun
The Pearly Everlastings run;
Never find enough to eat
But still they're plump and clean and neat.

WATER LILY
[Castalia Adorato]

Water Lily is a queen,
Wears sweet robes of white and green;
Sleeps so sweetly all night long,
Lulled by Green Frog's slumber song.

YELLOW POND LILY
[*Nymphaea Adrena*]

Yellow Pond Lily laughed and said,
"Some one splashed water on my head;"
Said Spotted Trout, "Perhaps t'was I
When I jumped out to catch a fly."

WATER ARUM
[*Calla Palustris*]

Water Arum shares his bog
With his good neighbor Mr. Frog;
Dressed in his best, when day time ends
The Frog's grand concert he attends.

COMMON MILK WEED
[Asclepias Syrica]

Said Common Milk Weed, "When I've fed
The bees, I put my babes to bed
In silken cradles, where they sway
Rocked by the little Winds all day.

BULL THISTLE
[*Cirsium Lanceolatum*]

Bull Thistle waves a thousand lances
So bugs and beetles take no chances;
But butterflies and honey bees
Are welcome any time they please.

COMMON MULLEIN
[Verbascum Thapsus]

Common Mullein's lots of fun,
He loves the children every one;
His velvet leaves when torn he'll lend
To any fairy who will mend.

BROAD LEAVED ARROW HEAD
[Sagittaria Latifolia]

Lovely Broad Leaved Arrow Head
Lives in Madame River's bed;
Loves to wade and splash all day
And with the Minnow children play.

LARGE PURPLE ORCHIS
[*Habenaria Fimbriata*]

Large Purple Orchis loves to grow
Where crowds of people do not go;
But you're quite welcome, if you'll tramp
To where she lives (It's rather damp).

THOROUGH-WORT
[*Rupatorium Perfoliatum*]

Said Thorough-Wort, "I used to be
Gathered to make a bitter tea;
So, I'm disliked, but I'll outlive it,
Now folks know better than to give it."

INDIAN PAINT BRUSH
[*Castilleja Coccinea*]

Indian Paint Brush holds his cup
Of brilliant scarlet petals up;
That's all he does; for he's a shirk
And lives on other people's work.

BLACK EYED SUSAN
[*Rudbeckia Hirta*]

Saucy Little Black-Eyed Susan
When her mother caught her snoozin',
Rubbed her sleepy eyes and said,
"Guess I'll toddle off to bed."

Weitere Ausmalbücher von Luisa Rose:

Titel	ISBN
Alice im Wunderland	9783741297502
Blumen und Märchen	9783743102002
Der Struwwelpeter	9783743102699
Die Struwwelliese	9783743102811
Don Quixote	9783743104037
Drei kleine Schweine	9783743104099
Eine Blumenhochzeit	9783743104105
Fröhliche Reigenspiele	9783743104112
Lustige Tanzspiele	9783743104273
Reise ins antike Griechenland	9783743112568
Flucht ins antike Griechenland	9783743112599
Pariser Leben im 19.Jahrhundert	9783743112704
Die Sommerkönigin	9783743112742
Der Schneider und die Krähe	9783743112827
Die Wikinger	9783743113275
Hänsel und Gretel	9783743114265
Max und Moritz	9783743103214
Schnurrdirburr	9783743112834
Mode des 18. und 19. Jahrhunderts	9783743112971
Kostümbilder des 18. und 19. Jahrhunderts	9783743114401
Abenteuer im Bienenland	9783743117051
Griechische Helden der Antike	9783743117709
Märchen alter Zeit	9783743116559
Wildblumen Kinder	9783743137707
Blumenfeen	9783743137738

Notizbücher von Luisa Rose:

Titel	ISBN
Drachentöter (Notizbuch)	9783743113077
Natures Wonders (Notizbuch)	9783743113817
Gedankenspiel Notizen (Notizbuch)	9783743113886
Smaragd Notizen (Notizbuch)	9783743114296
Jagd Notizen (Notizbuch)	9783743114302
Tradition (Notizbuch)	9783743114319
Antik Notizbuch (Notizbuch)	9783743114326
Veni Vidi Vici (Notizbuch)	9783743114340
Black List (Notizbuch)	9783743114371
Mystic Notes (Notizbuch)	9783743114388
Magic Notes (Notizbuch)	9783743114418
Fantasien (Notizbuch)	9783743114463
Creative Notes (Notizbuch)	9783743114487
Persönliche Notizen (Notizbuch)	9783743114494
Peter Pan (Notizbuch)	9783743114531
Rose (Notizbuch)	9783743114548
Quality Street (Notizbuch)	9783743114555
Rubin Notizen (Notizbuch)	9783743114647
Schmetterlinge (Notizbuch)	9783743114661
Ali Baba (Notizbuch)	9783743114678
The portrait of a Lady (Notizbuch)	9783743114692
Shakespeare (Notizbuch)	9783743114722
Brainstorming (Notizbuch)	9783743114739
Merlin (Notizbuch)	9783743114746
Rügen (Notizbuch)	9783743114784

Möchtest du über neue Bücher von Luisa Rose per email Informiert werden? Dann schicke eine Email mit ‚Newsletter' im Betreff an Luisa.Rose@t-online.de